Iron Alchemy of the Gods:

Feed Your Body with the Strength and Wisdom of Valhalla

Iron Alchemy of the Gods:
Feed Your Body with the Strength and Wisdom of Valhalla

RC Fordham

Honor the Roots
2016

First Printing: 2016

ISBN 9781520184104

Honor the Roots
421 Carter Avenue
Harriman, Tennessee 37748

www.HonorTheRoots.com

www.Instagram.com/HonorTheRoots

www.Facebook.com/HonorTheRoots

Contents

Introduction

This book is part philosophy and part work-out guide. It synthesizes the duality of both esoteric and exoteric practices. To effectively summarize the contents you will find here, we can say that the *Iron Alchemy of the Gods* is a handbook for the pagan soul and mind living life in a contemporary era, as well as a harbringer contributing to the revival of our ancient folkway. Following the footsteps of our Norse tradition, *Iron Alchemy of the Gods* has been crafted for Norse Heathens, Vikings, and Pagans who follow an undiluted iron philosophy of life. It is a shamanic warrior doctrine that promotes strength and knowledge as the two keys that open Odin's Gates.

In forging our pathway to the gods, we have discovered a secret way to achieve the worthiness of entrance into Asgard; it is a path that maximizes and fulfills our life here in Midgard. We offer in this book a pathway that is accessible to all folk in our modern era regardless of economic constraints or geographical placement. An ambitious character and a noble spirit are the only pre-requisites to attain the rewards of the *Iron Alchemy*. While you digest the contents found within this book you will be propelled a higher spiritual position than you ever have before.

Iron Alchemy of the Gods has a particular reader in mind. I have primarily written this book for those who understand the body as a key to finding a pathway to the gods and *Valhalla*. However, we address many things that all our folk will find helpful in their journey. Our attitude is simple, yet extremely radical in our current age of degeneration and vile decadence. Our motto is this: *We are going to make no apologies for what can be attained by the human body and mind!* <u>*We aim to become a weapon of the gods.*</u>

To attain what can be achieved with *the Iron Alchemy* you must have a steadfast desire for what is to come, for what is your birthright…. no matter what may be the cost. The path of the Iron Alchemy is one of struggle and pain. It requires a discipline that has receded and is mostly absent among men in the current Wolf Age, or better known in the current currents as the Kali Yuga. The *Iron Alchemy of the Gods* carves out a pathway to make mortals into heroes. Men will be born into heroes and heroes will be born into gods. No longer shall those within our religion pollute its revival with devolution. This book is about using the struggle of existence to become fully alive and reach your maximum potential. The *Iron Alchemy* is about growth.

We make no apologies for our desire of strength and abhorrence of weakness!

We make no apologies for the strength of our gods! Likewise we make no apologies for harnessing the power we find within ourselves. *OUR BODY AND OUR WILLS* are intimately connected. So it follows that a strong body is only a shroud over a stronger will. By turning our body into a vessel of pure strength, we put our will into flesh. By putting our will into flesh we make ourselves like our gods. In fact, as the 19th century philosopher Arthur Schopenhauer pointed out, there is no difference between our bodies and our wills. By developing a strong body we are developing a strong will.

BY FORGING A WILL AND BODY OF IRON WE MOLD OURSELVES LIKE THE WAR GODS WHO REIGN UP HIGH. THERE ODIN WILL GREET US AT THE GATES AS WORTHY OF HIS HALLS.

Chapter 1:

The Basics of the Iron Alchemy

All training starts from within your own being. Our training from the *Iron Alchemy* will have root in a warrior mentality. It is this frame that will be placed deep within your spiritual center. Once proper orientation of your mind is accomplished, the goal is then to move this reality outwards from your spiritual core. When unlocked, this force knows no limits. It goes beyond your innermost primordial being and permeates the human flesh. From the flesh it then is born into the exterior, everyday world. This force is your birthright and fate. It is your true essence. *"Know thyself,"* the ancients said. Take that into serious consideration. It is now time you learned your true nature.

Before the process of training can begin to come into the physical reality, you must first learn to conquer yourself. This battle is known as the greater spiritual war. The great dragon as our ancestors perceived it. This can only be accomplished through knowledge and discipline. Do not be fooled by modern semantics, the battle for the body is a spiritual war. It must begin there. You must show the body that mind will prevail. We have all heard *"mind over matter."*

Before now, you have let instinct run rampant. Its appetites have had no limits. The ugly truth of the matter is that you have followed the path of self-gratification – a sick and twisted egoism that gives nothing in return. It's all about choice. You have chosen the path of short term gratification over long term satisfaction. You have done this because you have followed the hedonistic urges of your body. As we will read, the *first pillar* of the Iron Alchemy states the flesh is your enemy. No, it is not endowed with sin as the Christian cosmology would behold as a first principle. Instead, it is made up of pure weakness. It is an all-consuming organism, without ever giving, without the knowledge of sacrifice. It does not practice Odin's holy example of self-sacrifice. You must understand this to progress with the *IRON ALCHEMY*. We will discuss more about sacrifice later on.

The fundamental condition of the human body is weakness. This knowledge, once realized makes it clear; the body is born weak and remains weak unless an inner change takes root. Infancy is only a condition that can be overcome with maturity. Without intervening action, the body is infantile, remaining so until it dies. If you allow this, you will live weak and be unworthy of the God's attention. You will remain unworthy of yourself. We are what we are, but that is not all we can be. Ego-gratification does not change this basic and fundamental fact of reality. In the gym, your body is weak against the force of the weight of the iron you lift. This is why training is not an option, it's a necessity. The body is the first thing to be conquered if you are to ascend to the gods. To subdue the weakness of the body is to participate in the holy war of the gods. With a never ending desire, your weakness must be sought to be obliterated.

Like the weakness of the material body, the iron you seek to lift with your body is also an enemy. It seeks to stop the flesh, to tire it, and to show the supremacy of weight and gravity against the machine of flesh and blood. Mostly, it wants to annihilate the will, restrain it, and make it submit. The weight is a messenger that tells you how weak you really are. In the grand scheme of things, it suggests that you are absolutely nothing. The harbinger tells you that you can not only control yourself but you have no control over your external environment.

All things are messengers, so learn to read the language. Our ancestors perceived all things as signs. Nothing was random and sporadic to them. That is only a symptom of our modern condition. Disconnected and drained from our spiritual core. Train yourself to see life this way, so that you may understand the language of higher powers, of beings, and the weaving created by the Norns. All events and circumstances in our life have meaning. Only fools think life is a random happenstance.

To complete the *Iron Alchemy,* you must learn to recognize the true nature of things. Gravity is your enemy. Like the giants who have declared war against the authority of Asgard over all things, likewise gravity has declared war against your own nobility and internal power. It is a proof of your own limits. For men who aspire to the divine aspirations of Asgard, gravity is the force that drags and destroys. To be firm and stand against gravity is to aspire to the gates of Odin's Hall. Only those who have broken the spell of it, champions who are no longer bound by their inherited weakness are allowed to feast next to the one-eyed god. All in all, training your body is a metaphor for the great spiritual war. You must drag that weight across the landscape. You must roll the boulder up the hill. You must suffer and learn to overcome the human condition.

Your will is the only thing that can transcend the weakness of the body and the eternal enemy of man's god-like aspirations; i.e. gravity. For this reason it is imperative to put the goal before the flesh at any cost. This is what it means to develop a warrior mindset. An internal recognition of the goal and your condition must be set.

Quod tu es, ego fui, quod ego sum, tu eris.
What you are I once was, what I am, you will become.

Every time there is growth there is struggle. From birth to death, all things are a struggle. Positive change requires overcoming inertia (*gravity*) while negative change requires giving into it. For every expansion, there is an equal and opposite effect of inertia. The Norse myths are fundamentally about the struggle for growth and expansion through the holy vehicle of Odin.

The Aesir: Celestial Gods of War

The Aesir are gods of *war and struggle*. They were the first to rule in Asgard before the Vanir joined them in inter-marriage. They are the principle elite and are those who will play an important role during Ragnarok. Among them:

- Odin
- Balder
- Freya
- Thor
- Tyr
- Ullr
- The Valkyries

It is underneath the banner of these gods and their cosmological vision for the universe that *Iron Alchemy* orients itself. Their vision of the world relays the cosmic reality of struggle. Nature is the ultimate testament to this truth, particular to ourselves and the gods. Their goal is to achieve growth through sacrifice. It is a vision that you must learn to cultivate and share with them. We show our allegiance to the Aesir, and they look favorably upon our deeds.

The deities who live in Asgard are very closely linked with the destiny of man. To visually portray this relationship we can say the gods are bound to our fate by the rune of Gebo (*pronounced geh-bo*). It is a rune of reciprocity, signifying that every exchange has an equal cost.

Gebo stems from the Indo-European root *gheb. This translates into "give" or "receive." Notice the two marks of equal porportions in the rune. These signify a balance or a sort of scale. In order to take, you must give something of equal value. This divine law as expressed in the rune gebo has been broken in our current times and is reason that Ragnarok is hastily coming. It is the outcome of the modern world.

Gebo is the rune of gifts, but also hidden within, it carries with it the aspect of being a rune of sacrifice. For every gift, there must be a sacrifice. No thing, no matter how misleading Loki can be in his trickery, is given for free. This is one of the reasons why the ancients held blots and offered to the gods what was theirs to take. These acts were not primitive as the maniacs in the current streams of anthropology suggest, but manifestation of a divine principle.

Beyond gifts and sacrifices, *Gebo* also represents an oath-exchange. It is the rune that binds oaths together and consecrates them in a divine manner. Another reason that the double lines intersect.

An example from the lore:

"Better not asked than over-sacrificed.
A gift always demands another gift as a payment.
Better not sent than over-wasted."

The interests of the *Aesir* reside primarily in their relationship with the cosmos and the defeat of their enemies. Odin acknowledged human's special place in this holy war recruiting the warrior elite to serve him as *Einherjar* during *Ragnarok*. All men are not created equal and not all men live equally.

Group and self sacrifice is a theme that the *Iron Alchemy* is clear about. Without it nothing can be achieved. The ego driven individual knows nothing other than selfishness. Selfishness has manifest itself at its totality in our society. It is a devolving energy and is only powerful in a world caught up in the material reality. Odin sought the security of his people for the future and he sought the knowledge required to participate in the struggle. Just as Odin dedicated his existence to self-sacrifice, we too shall sacrifice our lives to this struggle. Dedication to our religion is not a hobby, it is a lifestyle. Make it a full-time activity for it is the goal of our life in Midgard. However, do not be fooled into thinking that you cannot take what is yours to take.

Odin is my Master but I am my Lord

Harnessing the Runes of Power

Symbols serve as bastions of power for those who understand their proper usage. With a properly trained mind and a natural instinct for the spiritual and metaphysical world one can come to a proper understanding of why the Futhark runes were so revered by Odin and our ancestors. They serve us on many levels. Runes are tools of communication which come from the gods and the natural laws of nature.

With this in mind, we must also understand that the human mind must fixate itself upon objects in order to function properly. Odin seized the runes so that you would have the opportunity to use them for this purpose. The runes are tools for mortal ascension. We must relearn how to use them as our ancestors did. They are to be used to understand the mysteries and workings of the universe.

Before we go on, we must take a note. *The runes are not always divinatory objects as certain groups have led us to believe.* Such practice is part of a neo-mysticism which in no way match the reality. In fact, there is no evidence our ancestors used runes for divinatory work in the lore or literature. Instead, the runes are spiritual tools that lead to a deeper understanding of the higher self and the powers of the cosmos. Keep this in mind throughout the book.

What is desperately needed in our new generation is a true understanding of the runes. This journey is to be led by those with a spiritual capacity and no longer charlatans. This is to not say that our ancestors did not do divination work. But it is to say, we must be clear on what the runes are. They are windows to the inner workings of the universe and soul.

The purpose of the runes should now be clear. They were multi-faceted aspects of our ancestors and of the energies of the universe. They are more than just a static two-dimensional object. They are more than a material carving. They are some of the highest metaphysical substances. Every rune has its own being and personality. Each rune is exalted by the other. Together they support each other in a system. For example, let's use the image of a diamond. Each corner on its hard surface would represent a single rune. The gods also can be imagined the same way, but that is a discussion to be held in another book. That said, there are many runes which will be required in order to complete our full body transformation. The first of which is Uruz.

URUZ (UR)

The first rune which will be required to complete our full bodily and spiritual transformation is known as Uruz. Infamously, this rune corresponds with strength. It is the most potent rune that we will be dealing with in this book and the chosen symbol of the *Iron Alchemy* doctrine.

In the Anglicized world, we pronounce this rune by saying "ooo-rooze." While, currently the sound of this rune has dissolved amongst the English speaking peoples of our folk, it has retained some attachment and use within the modern German language (*Ur*). However, our goal, as English speakers, will be to revive it and give it life once again in the immediate future. We will become the necromancers of words. Understanding the language of Uruz will unlock the meaning of the rune and as I will show you below, we do have the keys to do so.

If we consider the variant rune name of *Ur*, we will be able to discover vestiges of the rune in our contemporary language. Vestiges that are hidden and obscure, but decodable. First, we must convert *Ur* to the English root *Or and Er*. Before we understand why this must be done, and what it means for the *Iron Alchemy*, let's examine Uruz's relationship with the Auroch.

An analysis of this rune's linguistic origins leads us to find it as an expression of the mighty Auroch (*The Aur-Ox or the Ur-Ox*), the now extinct European bison. This beast, having each horn measuring close to 3 feet, would stand nearly 6 feet tall in the ancient landscape. The distance between the tip of each horn could reach lengths of 12 feet. If such a reference is found in our linguistic record, it reveals the importance this beast played in the life of our ancestors. We must remember, our ancestors communicate to us through what they have left for us. One possible suggestion while dealing within in the scope of the Norse and Germanic tradition, shows Uruz as a possible reference to *Audhumbla*. This was the primordial cow central to the Norse Creation story.

The promulgation of the idea of a giant primordial bovine during creation is found not only in the Norse mythos, but also in many Indo-European traditions. The Celtics described the white bull of Ai, The Hindus mention the beast under the name of Yama. The early bovine is also found in Latin and Persian mythos. Altogether, a creation cow is found in 5 of the 11 significant language groups of the Indo-Europeans. This fact we must consider as important in the reconstruction of religion and in the quest to gain an accurate representation of our world. These types of insights will wrestle our civilization from the grip of the last 2000 years of a foreign religion that was forcefully grafted upon us.

Before we continue where we started to discuss some linguistic details concerning Uruz, look at the poetic representation of this rune:

> "Dross comes from bad iron;
> the reindeer often races over the frozen snow."

– Old Norwegian Rune Poem

Note: The reindeer here is interchangeable with the Auroch. The reason that it was not transcribed as so originally is because the bison had gone into a state of population decline. Its lack of being ever present in the northern landscape by the time our rune poem was written shows that no reference to the Auroch served the people of the time –it also suggests that by the time Christianity had taken its grip on the people, they were already in a state of decline.

One may ask, what does the reindeer (Auroch) often racing over the frozen snow have to do with this rune? It's quite simple. This rune is dealing with the concept of self-mastery. One aspect of Uruz is giving insight into the nature of being able to harness the world. The reindeer here has mastered travelling over an impossible landscape. Not only can it navigate upon the snow, but it "races" over it. This concept is the northern version of the eastern saying of "ride the tiger." A saying which emphasizes staying above the violent and chaotic forces, never letting them get the best of you. *Uruz*, like the saying of "ride the tiger," also has the concept of mounting hidden into it, which I will elaborate a little further below.

The first part of the poem states, *"dross comes from bad Iron."* Dross is essentially waste from the blacksmithing process. We can now also see that embedded deep within this rune is the imagery of forging. Dross comes from forging with bad iron. This can refer to circumstances, actions, beliefs, opinions, and individuals. Particularly iron is considering the soul as the metal to be smithed. He individual is the master of the forge. This poem and the rune Uruz is dealing with an inner alchemy of self-mastery and strength.

With the concepts from the rune poem fresh in our mind, we can now return to focus on the linguistic origins and ties of the rune Uruz. Let's investigate it deeper by taking a look into the sounds of the rune.

Uruz, and particularly in *Ur* -the shortened form of the rune, we discover the root *Or or *Er. *Or pertains to a condition of reality, while *Er describes a person that does something or an activity. Here it may be appropriate to meditate on words such as "origin," whose proper meaning means to set into motion.

"*Or-igin" contains the Proto-Indo European root *ergh- "to mount." Once again, we are seeing a relationship between Uruz and the Auroch forming by decoding the language of our times. By harnessing the Uruz rune we are able to mount the bull.

By breaking down the rune poem and examining connections in the language of the rune, we have unlocked 3 clear concepts out of the Uruz rune:

Mastering + Forging + Strength.

We all face the inertia that tries to hold us back whenever we try to start to do something. So what then, does the great bull have to do with this rune? It symbolizes a breaking through. It is the shattering of objects that hold us back.

If there is something holding you back, you must learn to grow. If there is not growth, then this holy principle does not exist. Without Uruz, without this principle we cannot transgress boundaries that keep us contained. If we cannot transgress these impeding barriers, we get stuck and soon inertia gets the best of us.

So far we have realized *Uruz* represents a creature of great power. The inverted "U" shape reminds us of the mighty European Auroch and is what our ancestors had in mind when expressing the rune. The rune creates images in the mind of transformation and growth. This rune is a positive force when harnessed correctly. But beware; this rune can also represent a negative force, especially through neglect of its power. It is a life force involved in the struggle to survive.

However, digesting the knowledge presented so far and orienting ourselves to this rune is not enough. We can study it and dissect it without ever achieving our goal of the *Iron Alchemy*. In order to practice this inner alchemy we must become the living and breathing rune of pure strength.

How to Master the Rune Uruz

With this energy, we are exposed to the very root force of the universe itself. It is the force which all things rest. It is the energy that holds things together. Uruz speaks to us and says to be strong. It wants us to force ourselves to the limits, and then push beyond what we formerly thought was impossible. Uruz, the rune of strength and power, must be harnessed.

The best way to learn the runes initially is to draw them and read about them. When drawing this particular rune, you make a statement that impacts the mind/body complex. It is a testimony to yourself and the gods. You acknowledge this holy principle, which even the gods adhere to. The manifestation of this rune leads to the realization of how we can become the masters of our reality. Its basis is the expansion of the soul and body. Drawing the rune however, only activates one aspect of our existence – that is the mental state and the acquisition of knowledge (self-experience).

Note: We must acknowledge that the separation of the soul and body started with the modern era, in particular, with the realm of modern and degenerative philosophy. Our goal, therefore, is to unify the two as it was the view held by our ancestors.

The Northern Religion relates one cosmic theme. That is, the eternal struggle of all things to survive. That is the true reality of the myths. In this universe, predatory forces are out there. Imagine the wolf, who takes down the calf, or goat. This predatory reality is an opposing force to us. The only way to defeat it, is through the rune of Uruz.

To master this rune, you must make meditation your absolute foundation. Meditation is the key to all esoteric practices and to forming a bridge to the powers of this rune. To affect change in this world and to change your reality you must have a connection with that power. Meditation builds that bridge.

Material reality exists at a lower wavelength than powers and energies. In fact, it can be seen as a misrepresentation of the world, or as our Vedic brothers call it, maya (illusion). This is not to say that material reality does not exist, but that it is only an internal condition that can be overcome.

Mastering this rune requires you to pay the price of time and energy. Commitment to yourself is the only way this will work. A gift requires a gift as the rune *Gebo* has shown us. Commitment takes a level of seriousness. The runes deserve respect. You must give your full attention. Working with the runes requires all aspects of yourself. Meditation is something you have to do if you want to initiate the full transforming power of the runes.

Meditation is the key because through it arrives the power to silence the inner narrator – the mind and words that appear from seemingly nowhere. Meditation opens yourself up to the potency of communication with the runes.

Another way to invoke Uruz is through a type of Yoga. The purpose of this activity is to increase the flexibility of the body and align it with the powers of the rune. The runic position imitating the rune Uruz goes as following: Stand straight up with the vertebrae aligned as vertically as possible. Take the hands and stretch them above the head. Now, we with one hand behind the other move the hands directly horizontal and in alignment with the face. Now, carry the motion down until you arrive with your hands spaced directly in front of your feet. The legs should be as straight as possible, the back sloping like the top of the Uruz rune, and the arms as straight as possible. Hold this position for 60 seconds. With the release of your last breath, slowly return to the original standing position. This technique should be practiced daily, preferably in the early morning hours and the evening hours.

Do not yet fret if you do not how to properly meditate yet. In the sections below we shall discuss how to accomplish this. For now, just reach out to the Rune and form a connection. Fixate the mind on the object and use what you already know. Take an active role in uncovering the meaning of this rune. Bridge the gap between you and this rune. Do not live as an island.

Before we move on let's take a look at another rune important to the *Iron Alchemy*. It bears the name Hagalaz. It is akin to the lightning that extends from Thor's mighty hammer and represents the power of a storm. When harnessed, it is particular to a certain type of being (i.e. a regal warrior). It represents the concentration of power into a particular place.

Hagalaz (Hail): The Second Rune of the Iron Alchemy

Hagalaz is the mother of all runes. Protection from hail and fire. Hagalaz represents a unity and balance in things. It is known as the cosmic seed. However, as powerful as it is in creation, It is also a powerful rune of destruction leading to chaos. Through chaos and crises Hagalaz leads to new beginnings and spiritual awakenings. Notice, that this particular version of the rune incorporates the Uruz design. This is not accidental. Sometimes Hagalaz is drawn with two descending lines. For purposes in the *Iron Alchemy* however, we will be using the Hagalaz with one decending line connecting the two erect staffs.

Note: We will be invoking the Elder futhark version of this rune. The Younger futhark incorporates a design that is more attune to a cosmic egg shape. However, the meanings are mostly the same, though degenerated through the affects of time.

Let's look at a rune poem to get a greater grasp of this rune:

Hail is the whitest of grain;
it is whirled from the vault of heaven
and is tossed about by gusts of wind
and then it melts into water.

-Anglo Saxon Rune Poem

The poem shows us dual aspects of Hagalaz. To unlock this, we can start with the poem's description of the rune. It begins with the image of hail. Hail as we know, is a *hardened* substance that is destructive. Soon it is revealed to being violently thrown around the sky. The poem ends with a calmer image of the hail melting into water.

From the poem, we can derive an embedded formula:

Hail (frozen, solid, stagnant, inert) + Movement/Heat = Water (flowing, moving)

With the application of heat the stagnant states become moving. We also unearth the nature of the "frozen" state. This frozen state is the same state we find in our creation story. Interesting enough, we see the application of fire. The creation story tells us that everything came into existence in the gap between these two primal substances. Somewhere between fire and ice we discover creation and a substance that is new. Application of heat to a solid substance leads to creation (*this is a metaphor for the soul – but likewise can be viewed macrocosmically as well*).

While discussing primal substances let us address an issue here I've seen from other authors which is worth acknowledging. Another tempting connection may see water as the key to giving life to all things. Included in this view would be the other substances of fire, earth, and air. However, we must avoid this typical neo-pagan model that is based on the Greco-Roman traditions. The Northern mythos, though akin to our brothers and sisters in the south, represents a different worldview. The primordial substances as they are stated in the lore consist of *Fire* and *Ice*. Thus, we can clarify that water as illustrated in the rune poem should be viewed as the life giving principle. A substance of water is a substance of life. It is flowing, moving, and able to react. Hagalaz contains the animating force.

The Anglo-Saxon rune poem claims Hagalaz begins as something destructive, but ends in something new and seemingly calmer. Hail destroys the weak. It has a theme of nature, and deeper scrapings of consciousness embedded within it.

What we can take away here is that the creative force in Hagalaz cannot be separated from the destructive force. They are in marriage with each other and part of the holy cycle. This makes Hagalaz a rune that is all encompassing. Connecting with this rune, leads to a fuller understanding of all things. Including the destructive power of nature.

Hagalaz allows that which is hindering to be washed away. This rune introduces a modification or a death of inertia, allowing growth and rebirth to take its way. Hagalaz is the eternal wheel turning.

Life + Death = REBIRTH

Hagalaz unchained can bear problems for the warrior in training and for someone unable to allow what is weak within to disintegrate. However, through discipline the destructive force of Hagalaz is subdued and used properly. *Hail* is a frozen structure that allows no growth and eventually leads to destruction. The *fire* contained within Hagalaz is the struggle of existence, which annihilates what has become useless, confining, and a burden to growth. Wisdom is the frame that directs its powerful raw energy. As such, it is as transformative as *Uruz* and goes hand in hand with those aspiring to forge a pathway to the gods.

Hagalaz is also the ninth rune, which bears an important significance in the *Iron Alchemy*. This significance is discussed in the workout *Aesir 9 Set Method* located in Chapter 3.

Hopefully I have led you to a deeper understanding of these two runes. Start to focus your mental attention to them. Draw them whenever a pen and some spare time meet together. They deserve your respect.  Spend time daily with a clear mental image of them in your being. They will invigorate your psychic energy. They are the runes of the *Iron Alchemy of the Gods*.

Practice with the Runes

The goal of the *Iron Alchemy* is to become these two living and breathing runes. But before such a holy transformation can take place, they must be placed within your being by your own will. Now we must orient ourselves to a position where the runes can be used in our lives.

In our current times, the distraction of the world remains a constant in our everyday exeprience. Unless an individual is awakened, the chain of this world is only broken by sleep and meditation. Sometimes severe partying as an act of a negation of life can also break this chain. This is a path that many esoteric leaders have called the left hand path. It is extremely feminine. Although effective, the *Iron Alchemy* suggests to stay oriented with the goal fully formed in the mind, and to break the chain with sobriety. The left-hand path is only for a certain esoteric user in mind. Let us go with another way.

Let me know speak a truth; if one is not realized within, then personal freedom is impossible and that person resembles an animal more than a human being. They only respond to the environment and never act as free agents. This is how the fates control the lives of men. The runes are tools that can be utilized to break this bondage.

To break the chain and insert the runes into the center of your soul, you must find time for solitude daily. Any place shall do, as long as the environment does not tinker with the mind. As your skills develop and the pineal gland is pried open by your own work, this rune work and meditation can be practiced even amidst the busiest environments. Before practicing with the runes it is suggested that the rune-master has adequate nutrition. This includes proper hydration, and the limited use of alcohol, tobacco, and other mind-altering substances.

To begin, close the eyes and get in tune with your body. Feel your heart thunder. There is a glory to the body. Enjoy the feeling of flowing blood that circulates throughout your entire organism. You are a manifestation of the life force. Feel the heat that occurs and radiates out from you. The heat that you feel is created by your own being.

Now it is time to depart our attention to another place. After a few moments turn your focus onto your breath. Fill the lungs in slowly for 9 seconds. Pause for an amount of time and release the breath for 9 more seconds. Proper breathing here will mean the belly is in a state of contraction and expansion with the lungs.

As you repeat this, notice how you become settled in your being. You become settled into the vessel that is your body. Lose awareness of everything that surrounds you. Lose awareness of everything but yourself.

Now continuing this process imagine that there is only your breath and the rune Uruz. With each breath in, you are consuming the rune into your lungs.

With each breath out, you are releasing any energy that is not related to this rune.

Continue this process until you feel saturated in the power of *Uruz*.

Advanced Runic Pineal Training

While the previous exercise focused on filling the lungs with the force of Uruz, we now want to do the same thing to invigorate and awaken our pineal gland.

Located between the eyes in the forehead, it has been called previously the "third eye." In our world, many forces exist who seek to calcify it and make it useless to you. Modern science denies that this gland has any useful purpose to the modern human. However, the *Iron Alchemy* will awaken it.

Now, with your eyes closed, focus your psychic energy onto the spot where the third eye is located. As you focus, you should be able to target its precise location. Once located, a sensation will arise. Feel the energy that is harnessed here.

Now, imagine that instead of breathing through your nose, it is your pineal gland that acts as the doorway for breathing. With each breath inward, bring it in through your third eye. Each breath outward is to leave through the bottom of your feet.

As this process happens Inhale the rune of choice (either Uruz or Hagalaz). Feel it saturating your entire body. Take the opposite and inverse of the rune out as your breath out. Continue this process until you can envision the rune within your being.

Keeping the Pack Strong

Strength is unconditional; either you wield it like Thor's mighty hammer Mjolnir or you do not have the capacity to do so. It is not for the weak of spirit, body, and mind. While some may naturally bear this torch, others will have to make a decision. You have to choose what you will become. Strength is not irrational, nor barbarically egotistic. Strength is about expansion. In fact, we can make the claim that the two are synonymous. Furthermore, expansion is a choice, otherwise to refuse so is to retract into weakness and dissolution. To have true strength is to wield the most deadly physical and SPIRITUAL weapon against the enemies of yourself, your tribe, and the gods.

To train your physical body is to gain knowledge of what it means to have a solid character. To train your body is to go through rigorous discipline. In order to become a true warrior one must be well equipped to defend himself and those around him. This training, however, is not only particular to the body itself. It penetrates all layers of the soul. Growing the body makes you something greater than you were. This also means it conditions your consciousness.

Iron Alchemy is about being prepared to be active if the situation comes and proves to be necessary. It is about capability and achieving potential. One must be prepared AND capable. A heathen warrior who is unprepared to do so, is not a true warrior at all.

We are only as strong as our weakest link. This means that we have an obligation to become as strong as we can. As such we are also obligated to ridicule weakness. In our current world, such a view is almost a criminal act. Those who attack it, however, do so to perpetuate their own weakness. It is a strategy that utilizes morality to hold the pack back. Other forces are also involved here, ones that pertain to a new world order and the institution of a new slave system. However, this is off topic for the purposes of this book.

The individuals who are weakness embodied; the individuals who want to downgrade the group through a false morality that is equivalent to the Christian morals of old are unprepared for Ragnarok. These feeble minded people pretend that the danger is not real. But it may be that the danger has not yet reached their door yet... all signs show that it is coming.

When I began my Iron Alchemy training I was only 129 lbs. However, through deeper contact with the runes and a strict warrior discipline I grew to new heights. When this picture was taken, I had reached 185 lbs. My strength had grown exponentially and the waters of my mind had been calmed. I had become a true weapon. My will was now able to carve paths that were not laid out in front of me.

Me before the Iron Alchemy Transition. Weight: 129 Lbs. Notice the weak stature and small limbs. I am undernourished, lethargic, and without pride. I do not even closely resemble the man on the page before.

Note by Request: Alter was built as a doorway into the woods. I would enter ritually as I would pursue daily journeys into the forest. The forest is much a metaphor for the modern world and the mind.

Ragnarok and the Wolf Age

A friend once told me that the gods were dead and we were in a new age without them. Perhaps, this is true and Ragnarok has already unfolded. Maybe the gods have died. Or perhaps, they remain inaccessible to men and women in our current civilizational cycle as base materialism runs rampant and spiritual attunement has been minimalized. Our eye for the gods has been saturated with the profane, and therefore closed indefinitely. Only those who develop strong relationships with the gods will know the answer.

Ragnarok is considered an inescapable fate as the All-Father has made clear. Odin even gave his eye, to prolong this process for as long as he was able to do so. Here we can assume that we have free will to a certain extent. Nonetheless,

Decay. Degeneration. Destruction. And eventually, Death are at our doorstep.

These four "D" words are the markers that define our world today. We are no doubt in the Wolf Age (Kali Yuga) as predicted to Odin by the infamous Sybil:

> *"Brother shall strike brother and both fall,*
> *Sisters' sons defiled with incest;*
> *Evil be on earth, an age of. whoredom,*
> *Of sharp sword-play and shields clashing*
> *A wind-age, a wolf-age till the world ruins:*
> *No man to another shall mercy show."*

- Volupsa

Take a look through the modern fantasy. The world has been ruined by the many forces at play today. Corporate interests and corrupted governments around the globe, including those working for the global system have purposefully eroded nations and peoples, stealing wealth along the way. Society has been reduced to a mass of numbers managed by the political class. The modern human has ingested hedonism, being content to consume and destroy each other. Honor has been replaced with degeneration, as the circus sideshow of modernity continues its parade of devaluing the human being. However, it cannot and will not last.

The wolf age reveals things that are in great opposition to the Norse way of life. The way of life our ancestors breathed and acted upon every day is negated by the modern world. Individualism feeds this inversion. Modernity has led the world to reduce people to merely cosmopolitan objects. The circus has come to town.

Despair against the forces that be is useless. Combatting the madness of the modern world is simple, but takes courage. You must know who your kin are. You must know who your folk are. This is the tie that will prevent the erosion. One must look at the fall as a landslide only. Stay out of the way and let it fall until it hits the bottom of the mountain. Unfortunately this is a challenge that you will have to meet alone.

It is clear that the world's attention has been turned to things that will bring Ragnarok quicker. Whether this is the perfection of the globalist system, mindless debates about rights and policies, increased tensions between the east and west, destabilization in the Middle East, matters little. There is nothing worth saving. There are no institutions to resurrect. There are no vestiges from the past that have not been deluded and desecrated.

A holistic approach to the problems of this world are not happening. Instead, we are in a cultural war of ideas vs other ideas. An idea that comes in the way of the new stampede of ideas is considered refuse. And there are very little opposition that can effectively fight the stampede.

This outcome, however, should not be that surprising. Christianity poisoned our people by infecting us with a definition of truth that is supposedly universal. Even with the death of the religion, as is apparent now, its vestiges still have captured the hearts and minds of our folk. Truth, however, exists in a multiplicity and contradictions. It exists in layers. Truth depends upon the experiencer and varies between person and person. This is apparent in the world's different religions and cultures. This is apparent in truth as you have known it as a child,versus how you understand it now.

There is only one victorious end-game in the Wolf Age. That path is created by knowing yourself. The only way to know thyself is through the ancestors. Particularly what the ancestors spoke about. The Norse Lore tells us about their essence. The mythos communicates us with. To erase the world that we have been fed and to re-emerge ourselves in their world is the only way to survive the horrific wolf age. Afterall, their blood is flowing in your veins.

By becoming a *weapon of the gods* we are choosing to side with Odin's celestial vision of the cosmos. It is a pure act of rebellion in the final age of our civilization. We laugh in death's face —calm and collected we welcome the challenge. If Ragnarok is indeed upon us, it is imperative to get prepared and do the great work. Even if death takes us, we shall not be plunged into the great primordial abyss. By strengthening our person we are reinforcing the great gift of Hoenir, who along with Odin created humans. The gift of reason, persona, and individual consciousness is not to be discarded, let alone given up under any circumstance.

The way to attain Valhalla begins in Midgard. And in our fourth and final age (Wolf Age) before the rebirth of gods and men, the best place to start is with the body. Through the body we honor the ancestors. Through the body, we are ancestors in training. Through the body we keep our mythos alive. We shall do what is necessary to accomplish this.

In the final age, people will not adhere to the truth. Instead they will seek only those who will repeat what it is they want to hear. That is certainly the case now. That is why truth is so easily reconstructed and misrepresented. The gate keepers are able to narrate any world vision they deem necessary for your enslavement.

Surt with the bane of branches comes
From the south, on his sword the sun of the Valgods,
Crags topple, the crone falls headlong,
Men tread Hel's road, the Heavens split open.

A further woe falls upon Hlin
As Odhinn comes forth to fight the wolf;
The killer of Beli battles with Surt:
Now shall fall Frigga's beloved.

Surt was a Jotnar. The Jotnar are preconscious forces that are destructive and chaotic. Surt was from Muspelheim, the world of fire.

Odin comes forth to fight Fenris. Odin knows that he will fail, but continues to attack. He sacrifices himself, to give himself to all that he is trying to defend.

The fact that Odin dies in Ragnarok reveal a particular reality present in the Norse Myths that is not present in other European mythos. Our gods die. Our gods collectively experience Ragnarok with us. This means all things are connected. However, this is not to mean we are one. Do not be misled by the new age message of "oneness." Life is a vertical matrix of those who are greater than you and those who are lesser than you, it is not a horizontal one.

The Pillars of the Iron Alchemy

1. The flesh is born weak and remains weak unless something is done.

2. Gravity is an enemy of all men and true gods.

3. Discipline is the weapon that obliterates these two obstacles.

4. Training begins inward before it can permeate the flesh.

5. Only by becoming living runes can we transcend the mundane world.

6. Long term satisfaction must take the place of short term gratification.

7. The values of modern 'civil'-ization are base and devoid of true meaning.

8. Harnessing the body and mind forges a pathway to the gods.

9. Odin is lord, but I am my own master.

Chapter 2: Valhalla's Gym

Don't leave your weapons lying about behind your back in a field;
You never know when you may need all of sudden your spear.

Knowledge of the Body

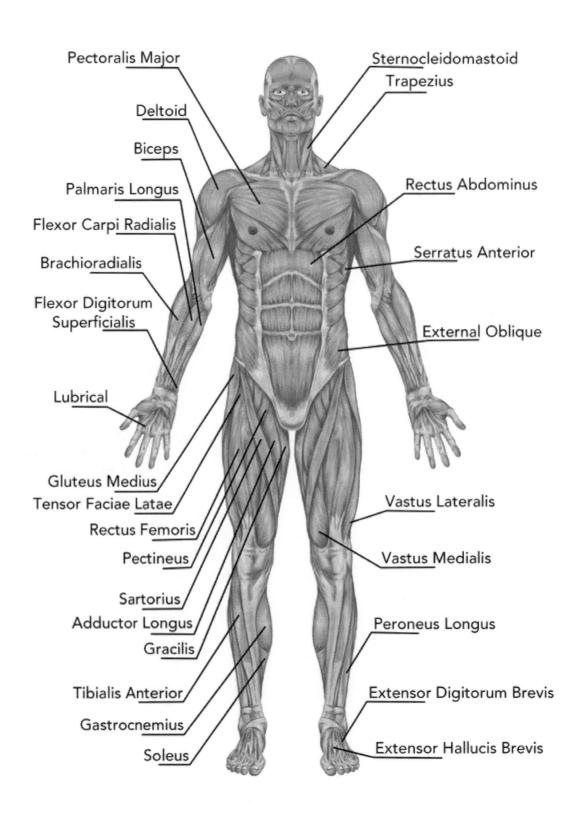

Pectoralis Major

Deltoid

Biceps

Palmaris Longus

Flexor Carpi Radialis

Brachioradialis

Flexor Digitorum
Superficialis

Lubrical

Gluteus Medius
Tensor Faciae Latae
Rectus Femoris
Pectineus
Sartorius
Adductor Longus
Gracilis
Tibialis Anterior
Gastrocnemius
Soleus

Sternocleidomastoid
Trapezius

Rectus Abdominus

Serratus Anterior

External Oblique

Vastus Lateralis

Vastus Medialis

Peroneus Longus

Extensor Digitorum Brevis

Extensor Hallucis Brevis

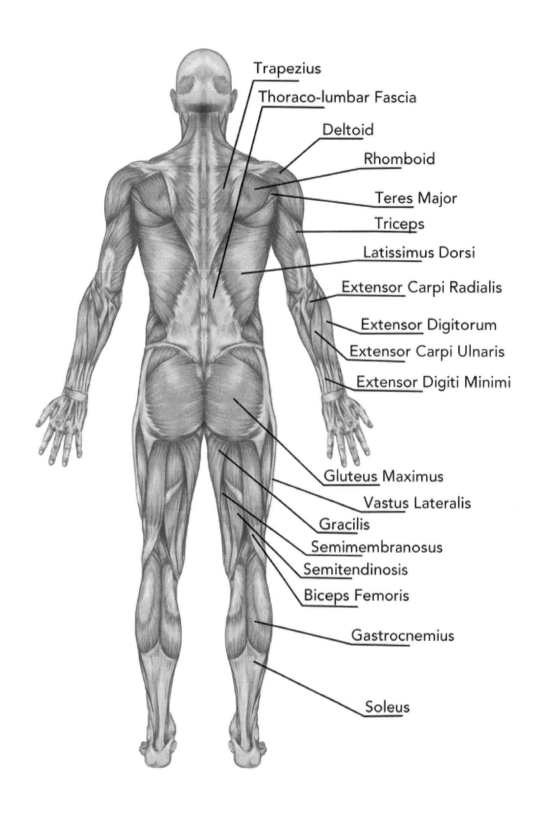

Trapezius

Thoraco-lumbar Fascia

Deltoid

Rhomboid

Teres Major

Triceps

Latissimus Dorsi

Extensor Carpi Radialis

Extensor Digitorum

Extensor Carpi Ulnaris

Extensor Digiti Minimi

Gluteus Maximus

Vastus Lateralis

Gracilis

Semimembranosus

Semitendinosis

Biceps Femoris

Gastrocnemius

Soleus

The Deadlift: Lifting The Mountain

Starting Position:

Ending Position:

The Deadlift is the most essential exercise for anyone looking to improve their strength and physique. It's going to work your entire body. For this reason it should be utilized vigorously. This exercise is used to pick up mountains. This metaphor you should have in mind when doing the deadlift.

TIP: LIFTING HEAVY IS FOR THE GODS. ALWAYS AIM TO DEADLIFT HEAVY.

Altering your form with deadlift variations will also change the emphasis on each muscle group. These you will discover as your progress in your routine. Over time you should experiment with this and discover the new gains to be had with each shift in the legs and body.

To successfully do the Deadlift requires skill and patience, but once the form is right you will have obtained a kingly status. The next thing to do is to make the weight heavy.

How to Do It:

- •Start with your feet directly under your shoulders.
- •Grasp the Bar with one hand over and one hand under.
- •Bend your knees until you make contact with the bar, but keep your knees over your feet.
- •Lift the Bar initially with your chest.
- •Keep moving up, but now pull with your back.
- •The top position should have your knees and hips locked. Do not go backwards with the bar.
- •Return the bar to the floor.

Muscles Worked:

Lower Back, Calves, Forearms, Glutes, Hamstrings,
Lats, Middle Back, Quadriceps, Traps

𝔖𝔮𝔲𝔞𝔱𝔰

Starting Position:

Always breathe in during the decent on the Squat movement. When rising back up to the starting position breathe out. This is where the rune breathing exercises in Chapter 1 become particularly useful. Use them as you practice these exercises.

Ending Position:

Squats are like putting the weight of the world on your shoulders. You'll want to get your ass as close to the ground as possible before starting the movement back up.

Squats charge the power in your ass, your hips and thighs, as well as your quads and hamstrings. Additionally, your skeletal system is strengthened, and the ligaments and tendons that run upwards attaching your muscles and bones. The lower half of your body is the most important part. Have a disciplined focus on this when beginning the training.

Tip: Where you put your feet is going to make a big difference on how this exercise is going to work your body.

Doing these will put your body into an anabolic state, which will transform your body, affecting all muscle growth and transforming your body into a vessel of pure and unbridled strength. This is essential in our full body transformation. We must become the living and breathing URUZ rune.

How to Do It:

- Grasp Bar with hands facing out.
- Keep your knees a little further than shoulder width.
- Place the Bar onto the top of your traps or further down onto your upper back.
- Descend keeping your head facing forward and not allowing your knees to go past your feet.
- Don't stop. Balance the weight and bring your ass to as close as the floor as you can.
- Return to the starting position.

Muscles Worked:

Quads, Calves, Glutes, Hamstrings, Lower Back

Bench Press

Starting Position:

Ending Position:

When the world falls on you, you will need to be prepared to push back. The bench press is just for that. You can do this one light or heavy depending on your own goals. If you go with light weight, you will need to go for maximum volume to get the same results that a heavy bench press will create.

Tip: The Bench Press is going to not only increase the size of your chest muscles, but also your front shoulder and triceps.

This is going to be the work out that builds a thick and robust chest suitable for the warrior elite.

While Deadlifts and Squats work the under world that consists of your lower body, the bench press does the same for your upper body.

How to Do It:

• Start with your hands past the width of your shoulders. A wider grip fully engages the pectoral muscles for maximum growth. Reducing the width of your hands, while working the inner of your chest, redistributes the weight to your triceps more than what is desirable.
• Lift the bar off the rack and move it over your chest.
• Breath out while dropping the bar down until it reaches your chest.
• Begin to exhale as you push the bar back up to its original starting position.

Muscles Worked:

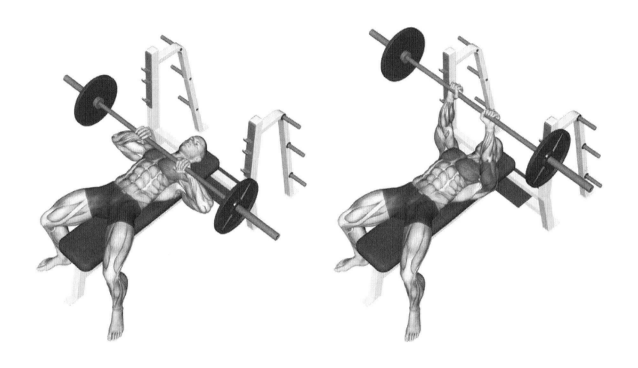

Chest, Shoulders, Triceps

Lat Pull-Down and Pull-up

The Lateral Pull Down, *ending position:*

Pull Up, *ending position:*

SOMETIMES YOU WILL BE KNOCKED OFF YOUR FEET. When this happens you will need to must your strength to pull yourself back up. NOTICE THE CHIN ABOVE THE BAR ON EACH ONE.

These two workouts are going to develop a massive back that will give you the capability of scaling the mountains of Jotunheim. Not only is the back affected, but so are your biceps.

While the Bench-press is going to primarily focus on the upper front of your body, these two are going to do the same for your dorsal side.

The amount of pull-ups you can do is a statement of not only your health and fitness level, but also your warrior level. A man who cannot do them is not capable of running with the heathen pack.

KEY POINTS:

•The main thing you want to remember with these two workouts is to keep your hands far apart. That is the only way to develop the massive wings you see on very large guys. That is exactly what you want to develop.
•Whether pulling the bar down or lifting yourself up, you are going to want to make sure that in the ending position your chin is over the bar. Not being able to do so implies you are lifting more weight than you can handle. This is going to result in poor form. Poor form is the enemy of the gods.
•Another mistake beginners often make is not using the back to do these workouts. Instead they will utilize the strength of the biceps. You should be able to tell the difference when you do this exercise. Fully engage your back muscles and clench them together. Feel it and you are doing it right.
•Never allow your elbows to lock out when performing either of these.

Muscles Worked, *Lat Pulldown*:

Lats, Biceps, Mid-back, Shoulders

Muscles Worked, *Pull Up*:

Lats, Biceps, Mid-back

Shoulder Press

Starting Position:

Ending Position:

Shoulders are the way other men and women gauge your physical status. Without a set of strong shoulders you will appear weak and feeble. Massive shoulders communicate massive strength and reveal an overall well-formed man.

As you can see, pushing the weight of the world above you with your shoulder muscles also works your triceps. Other various muscles are also engaged as this workout requires stabilization muscles to grasp and hold the weight.

How to Do It:

•Start with two dumbbells resting on your knees as you are seated.
•Lifting one weight at a time, use your legs to bring each dumbbell to your shoulders. Rest the weights there.
•With your palms facing outward, breath out and push the weights simultaneously up.
•Your hands should drive in a straight line upward. This is the key to good form.
•Push until your arms are fully extended.
•Breath in and return the weights down. This time do not return the weights to your shoulders. Your palms should be parallel to your mouth.

Like the squat, there are many variations to the shoulder press. Each one will have a different affect upon your body. Utilize them to fix inconsistencies and weak areas as they develop.

Muscles Worked:

Shoulders, Triceps

Dumbbell Lateral Raise

Starting Position:

Ending Position:

The shoulders have a variety of movement. In order to get them to the warrior-level of robust, you need to supplement your shoulder press. *Lateral Raises* will widen your shoulders.

TIP: The lateral raises work not only the deltoid, but the triceps and the traps.

However, if you feeling this exercise in your neck you are doing something wrong. Instead of focusing the weight into your shoulder you are dispersing it into your traps. There are other workouts for this, so to do so is counter-productive. When this happens lower the weight or shift your form until you can feel it working where it is supposed to. A shoulder injury is overly devestating so be sure that you are doing the shoulder workouts right.

How to Do It:

- Choose a lighter size dumbbell. Lifting heavy on this workout is going to destroy your form and thus it will obliterate the effectiveness of this exercise.
- Start holding the dumbbells either in front of you or beside your hips.
- Lift the weights with your shoulders, keeping the weights slightly in front of your body.
- Do not lock your elbows completely out.
- When you reach the top of your position make sure your hands are slightly tilted forward as if you are pouring a glass of water out.
- Return the weights to the starting position.

Muscles Worked:

Shoulders

Shrugs

Starting Position:

Ending Position:

Without working your trapezius you will have a small neck. Your large muscles will appear as a monstrosity and you will lack symmetry of the gods. Shrugs remedy that for a divine ascetic.

When doing shrugs not only will you be working your traps, but if the weight is heavy enough you will be engaging your forearms.

The key here is to do a lower weight a lot of times, or try to do a heavier weight and sustain the ending position for as long as possible.

TIP: Hold the shrug position for as long as possible with as much weight as your arms can carry. This static hold will demolish your traps and build massive forearms.

Muscles Worked:

Traps, Forearms

Curls

Dumbbell Curl, *starting & ending positions*:

Hammer Curl, *ending position*:

Barbell Curl, *starting position:*

Massive *Biceps* add impressive aesthetics to the power residing in the rest of your body. Big arms can wield big and heavy weapons.

SEATED DUMBBELL CURLS:

- Place yourself seated onto a bench with with two dumbbells in your hands.
- Maintain a straight back and keep the face staring straight ahead.
- Start with the dumbbells at arm's length with your palms facing in.
- Begin to force the dumbbell up only using the power within your bicep.
- Turn your wrist once the dumbells ascend past your thighs.
- At the top of the position squeeze your biceps hard!
- Slowly lower the dumbbells to the starting position.

PREACHER CURLS:

For this exercise your gym will need a preacher curl bench although modifications can remedy the lack of your gym having one.

- Sit at the end of the weight bench with the feet firmly rooted on the floor.
- Using a shoulder width grip, grasp the loaded bar in both hands not letting your wrists curl downward.
- With your biceps force the bar upward towards your shoulders in a movement that resembles an arc.
- Bring the bar up to your chin and squeeze the biceps hard!
- Lower the bar slower than you brought it up to get maximum work for each rep.

Muscles Worked

Biceps, Forearms

Tricep Pushdown

Starting Position:

Ending Position:

While your triceps are going to get a heavy dose from other workouts you will need to supplement it with these. Often I imagine shoving my enemy into the ground when doing this exercise. The vivid imagery provides an extra boost of energy.

A lot of the workouts we have discussed are going to hit your triceps. However, it's still important to supplement your routine with these workouts which primarily engage the triceps. When you strengthen your triceps, you are going to have more power to do your compound exercises such as the Bench Press.

Muscles Worked, *dumbbell triceps extension*

Triceps

Chapter 3: Workouts of Asgard

Aesir 9 Set Method

The most brutal training method I offer in the *Iron Alchemy* is the *Aesir 9 Set Method*. In my experience I have been able to pack on 10 pounds of muscle in a 12 week cycle using this *Iron Alchemy* workout. For this reason it is my favorite. It destroys plateaus and forges new pathways up the body building mountain towards Asgard. The workout will blow up your muscles like a balloon, so prepare yourself mentally for the devastating effect of hypertrophy. With this workout, Asgard is in your sights.

The secret to the *Aesir 9 Set Method* is in the number 9. Our ancestors recognized this as a holy number related to sacrifice. To illustrate, Adam of Bremen writes:

"A general festival for all the provinces of Sweden is customarily held at Uppsala every nine years. Participation in this festival is required of everyone. Kings and their subjects, collectively and individually, send their gifts to Uppsala; - and – a thing more cruel than any punishment – those who have already adopted Christianity buy themselves off from these ceremonies. The sacrifice is as follows; of every kind of male creature, nine victims are offered. By the blood of these creatures it is the custom to appease the gods. Their bodies, moreover, are hanged in a grove which is adjacent to the temple. This grove is so sacred to the people that the separate trees in it are believed to be holy because of the death or putrefaction of the sacrificial victims. There even dogs and horses hang beside human beings. (A certain Christian told me that he had seen seventy-two of their bodies hanging up together.) The incantations, however, which are usually sung in the performance of a libation of this kind are numerous and disgraceful, and it is better not to speak of them."

Basics of the Workout:

How Long to Rest: 60 to 90 seconds.
Tempo of Each Rep: 4 – 0 – 2
Suggested Rest Days: For each workout day follow it with a day of rest. If undergoing an extensive workout regimen you can do the first two workouts back to back. Just be sure to get plenty of rest as it plays a key part in muscle repair after hypertrophy.

Workout 1: Upper Body

MAIN EXERCISES

Dumbell or Barbell Bench Press:
- 9 sets @ 9 reps.
- Rest 90 seconds between each set.

Pull ups or Lat Pull Downs:
- 9 sets @ 9 reps.
- Rest 90 seconds between each set.

SUPPLEMENTAL EXERCISES
Cable Chest Flys:
- 3 sets @ 9 reps each.
- Rest 90 seconds between each set.
- Follow last set with a drop set until muscle failure.

Bent-Over Barbell Row
- 3 sets @ 9 reps each.
- Rest 90 seconds between each set.
- Follow last set with a drop set until muscle failure

Workout 2: Lower Body

Main Exercises

Squat:
- 9 sets @ 9 reps each.
- Rest 90 seconds between each rep.

Deadlift:
- 9 sets @ 9 reps each.
- Rest 90 seconds between each rep.

Supplemental Exercises
Seated or Machine Calf-Raises:
- 3 sets @ 9 reps each.
- Rest 90 seconds between each rep.
- Follow last set with a drop set until failure.

Workout 3: Additional Body Parts

Main Exercises

Tricep Pushdown or Press:
- 9 sets @ 9 reps each.
- Rest 90 seconds between each rep.

Hammer Curls:
- 9 sets @ 9 reps each.
- Rest 90 seconds between each rep.

Shoulder Press or Variation
- 9 sets @ 9 reps each
- Rest 90 seconds between each rep.

SPECIAL NOTE:

If workout 3 takes too long or is too strenuous consider creating a 4th workout day for shoulders alone. If you decide to do this you will need to attack abs at the end of the shoulder workout.*

The Natural Method

Weights are a modern convenience. In some way, they are also barrier. The gym is limited in the way it helps develop the body. While weight training is excellent for aesthetics, true strength is cultivated through movements and exercises that engage the entire fabric of the bodily structure. We won't go into detail here. Let's go right into the workout.

Chapter 4: Feasting in Odin's Halls

A HEAVY DIET OF PROTEIN IS THE ONLY THING SUITABLE FOR AN ELITE WARRIOR. The ancestors knew. PROTEIN IS THE KEY.

The Keys of a Diet of a God

While mead and ale is a drink for gods and men alike, there is more to the diet that forges a pathway to Valhalla. Only the elite warrior class of our ancestors were privileged enough to eat meat. Slaves, peasants, and those belonging to the lower classes of society were not given the privilege, and more often than not, it was illegal for their consumption of it. Eating meat without permission could warrant the death penalty. This shows how our ancestors thought of protein as an elite food that was reserved primarily for the warrior class.

Today, however, things have changed. The modern era, beyond the breaking down of the ancient barriers of class, has ensured that sources of protein are everywhere and available to everybody. While everyone's body chemistry is different and has differing demands, one thing remains true for everyone; a warrior must consume lots of meat in order to get the body to grow into a vessel of pure and unbridled strength.

The Initial Keys are as Follows:

- Drink a lot of water (*Mead/Ale is acceptable in moderation*)

- Milk is also acceptable, it's a powerhouse of nutrients. •Follow G.O.M.A.D. if you are not already over weight/lactose intolerant. This means drink a Gallon of Milk a Day. Do it. Live by it. You will grow. (*Our ancestors revered the great primal cow*)

- Eat food that is in season and as raw as possible. This is how our ancestors ate and by doing this you will gain more energy and health than is possible with pasteurized and processed foods.

- •Eat large meals that consist of primarily protein. This is to be the focus of all your food consumption. I choose to eat steak and eggs daily. It's not as expensive as it sounds. DO NOT focus your diet on protein shakes. Steak and Eggs is always better.

- Do Not Eat Food that is bad for you. Snacks and meals without protein are completely out. Don't put useless shit in your body.

The fact of the matter is the world of nutrition has fundamentally changed – to our advantage. While the politics and economic charades hinder us from eating food that is still energized with life, we do have access to more than ever before. Use this to your benefit. Invest in yourself with wise foods.

Your eating plan should be as simple as possible. Everyone who wants you to add up protein and carbs and split your meals is full of bullshit. That belongs to an industry who wants only your money. They do this so you will buy the latest trending supplement and diet book. You need to learn the skill of trusting yourself. Your gut is often called your second brain for a reason. You are going to have to trust yourself on when you need to eat and on how much to eat. Habits will ensure that you cultivate a will to pick foods that are good for you.

You will never go wrong following these simple rules. But the question remains, how did our ancestors eat?

The Viking Dietary Habits

Sources for a proper diet do not begin to be recorded until the late medieval era, the 1300's to be exact. While our ancestors had been converted into knights under the banner of Christianity, I think we are safe to assume that their diet fundamentally remained unchanged, although evidence suggest that the late medieval period changed the southern Germanic and northern tribes diet from protein based into cereal and grain based.

Let's begin with how many times a day our ancestors ate. The custom of the era was to eat two large meals a day. The first meal was known as the *dagmál*, or literally, "day-meal." This meal was eaten a few hours into the working day. It is what we today would call breakfast. It was a large and hearty meal meant to fuel people until the late afternoon and evening.

The second meal came much later in the day. Usually 10 to 12 hours after the dagmál. The Vikings called this meal *náttmál*. It is the equivalent of what we would call dinner.

As you see our ancestors did not eat as we do today. To this day, I follow these two meal times as was lived by our ancestors. I eat two large meals daily, with perhaps a few snacks in between. They developed this system to work with the natural structure of the body. Listen to the body and I think you will find the same rhythm within.

Meat and Dairy Products

Our ancestors were only able to eat food that was grown within their own geographical area. However, extensive trade networks ensured that food not grown in the northern countries was available.

Large varieties of protein were available to the Vikings. Beef, Pork, Lamb, Deer, Geese, Duck, Fish, and Goat were staples to everyday life. However, consumption of meat was limited due to seasonal changes that impacted farming.

Cows were the most important livestock to the Vikings. This was not due to the fact that their meat was highly valued. Instead, their ability to produce dairy products made them an appreciated animal. Cattle were more valued than gold and other precious metals. Take a look at the runic word "fehu." This literally means wealth and gold. The root "fe" means cattle. Cattle were the most important part of everyday life and the economic system of the Vikings. This, however, is not to say they did not consume their meat products.

The consumption of milk was rare in these times. Milk was more renown for what could be made from it. Immediately after milk was acquired the northern people converted it into skyr or cheese. From here, it kept a shelf life of many months, and would be used to develop more products such as butter.

Slaughter of livestock usually began in the late fall / early winter months. While most meat items were a seasonal dietary item, our ancestors had devised ways to preserve it. When dried properly, meat products had the ability to stay edible for many years. There were also other methods like smoking and fermenting. While larger animals were seasonal, certain kinds of livestock like birds were slaughtered year round to ensure a holistic diet in non-seasonal months.

Wild animals such as deer, reindeer, squirrel, and elk were also eaten, but in much smaller portions. This kind of meat was usually preserved for the nobles. Hunting wild game in their forests was strictly prohibited by law. Hunting was an activity reserved for the elite of society. Fishing however, was largely practiced and made up a significant portion of the everyday diet. Some scholars have estimated that 25% of protein consumption in Viking society came from the seas and rivers. This figure also includes the consumption of shellfish.

Fruits, Vegetables, and Spices

A holistic diet cannot be based on protein alone. While our ancestors ate large amounts, their nutrition was balanced by other categories on the food pyramid. This excludes breads and grains. This category entered the common diet less than a thousand years ago and was rarely found in archeological sites of the Vikings. When grown, they were mostly used to make ales. Alcohol played an important role in the winter months, making up for the lack of carbohydrates in the diet that included fresh fruits and vegetables.

Our ancestors ate incredible amounts of berries. These include blackberries, strawberries, blueberries, cherries and more. They were also fond of fruits found on trees such as apples and plums.

The Vikings were also able to acquire fruits from distant lands. Thanks to extensive trade networks established by early explorers, figs and grapes were commonly imported from Southern Europe and in the Middle East. Like meat, fruits were able to be preserved for long amounts of time through drying.

Vegetables were also consumed in large amounts. These were acquired through farming and gathering practices. Beets, Onions, Beans, Carrots, Spinach, and Mushrooms have all been found in archeological sites across Northern Europe. During famines and times with very sparse food storage, acorns were also accumulated to be eaten, however this practice was rare.

While Vikings ate very well, they also knew how to spice up their diet with herbs. The following items have been found in early Viking archaeological sites: black mustard, coriander, cumin, dill, fennel, garlic, hops, horseradish, juniper berries, lovage, marjoram, mint, mustard, parsley, poppyseed, thyme, watercress, wild caraway. It is certain that shamans also used herbs for medicinal purposes. As well, scholars have argued the Berserkers often ate Amanita Muscaria, commonly known as the fly agaric or fly amanita. Ingestion of this mushroom, along with large amounts of alcohol would have other worldly effects on the battlefield.

As the Vikings grew and their conquest spread out, extensive trading routes brought in even more exotic spices. Pepper, cumin, ginger, nutmeg, and cloves were all assimilated into the diet after their acquisition was made in distant lands.

Now that we have a basic understanding of our ancestors diet, the next section is designed for the wisdom seeker who wants to know more about the basic processes of the body, modern science, and how this all ties into the *Iron Alchemy of the Gods*.

Food of the Gods

Food is very important in the *Iron Alchemy of the Gods* program. Without proper nourishment we would fail to translate our wills into this material world. However, we are against becoming so particular with our foods that an improper attitude belonging to the bourgeoisie class develops. Yet, without the knowledge of how food works in our own bodies, every attempt to conquer ourselves would be in vain.

In order to operate like a Viking-god, you need calories. Calories are tiny bits of energy that your body uses to perform work. Counting calories isn't as important as knowing what calories will be the best ones to consume for the maximum effect on your workout.

Carbs

FORGING A PATHWAY ᛃ TO THE GODS ᛃ

Carbohydrates are essential to supplying the body with its desire to have glucose. Glucose is then converted and stored into your muscles and liver as glycogen.

Glycogen is potential for energy that is stored in the reservoirs of the body's muscular system. As muscles are pumped full with glycogen, they take on a robust appearance.

Your body's need for glucose can also have a detrimental effect upon your workout program. If you are lacking an adequate amount in your body, it will then make the decision to break down proteins within your system. It does this in order to supply the brain with energy and create new blood cells.

If you want to stop this, then eat your carbs. However, if you want to be like the ancestors large amounts of protein will do.

Protein

As we mentioned before, to craft a body worthy of entry into Asgard, you are going to need to consume a large amount of proteins daily. Proteins are made up of smaller building blocks called amino acids in much of the same way that glucose is the foundation for what is a carbohydrate.

There is an intimate relationship between proteins and nitrogen which are of consequence to those seeking to become a *weapon of the gods.*

For example, if your body excretes more nitrogen then what it is consuming, then it shall take upon the role of breaking down muscle tissue to get it. This state is known as being **anabolic.** On the other hand, if your body is consuming more than it is losing, you will be in a **catabolic** state.

To maintain an upper hand in this balancing war, eat foods that are rich in *nitrogen* such as meat, poultry, fish, and other seafood. This is why the rule comes about that states you should eat as much protein in grams conversely with the amount of weight you are in pounds.

Fats

While we mentioned glucose as being a source of energy for your muscles, the primary source of energy that your body uses is in *fats*. These combine with glucose, alleviating the burden of the body having to use protein as an energy source.

The best fats that contribute to this process are unsaturated fats. The greatest way to get this is to assimilate a large amount of avocados and nuts into your diet. Another way to include unsaturated fats into your diet is to cook with oils like canola or olive.

Supplementing a Warrior's Body

Supplements are a choice many warriors will choose to go about when crafting their heathen body. They are optional and in no way required to obtain a good physique. However, if you want an extra push to the threshold of your potential, you may want to consider consolidating them into your lifestyle.

Creatine

Creatine is naturally found within the contents of meat. If you are taking in lots of protein, you are already getting a steady amount. Creatine is also produced within the body's organism from the three amino acids known as glycine, arginine, and methionine. The kidneys, liver, and pancreas are the organs that produce it.

Creatine is used for the synthesis of ATP. Adenosine triphosphate (ATP), is the "energy" that powers the muscles. With all the lengthy science aside, choosing to supplement with Creatine is going to allow your body an upper-hand in the regeneration of ATP, maximizing your own human potential.

Glutamine

Glutamine is an additional supplement that those under taking the *Iron Alchemy* may want to consider.

Glutamine is a type of amino acid that is synthesized by the body. It can be found within the skeletal muscles, brain, lungs, liver, and stomach. It plays an important role in moving nitrogen around within the body. It is easily found in a variety of foods that a body builder is already consuming.

The choice of using these supplements are completely up to you. As I mentioned, these are found in a healthy diet, and therefore are not essential to the *Iron Alchemy*. However, for those wanting to push past the plateaus of idle gains, they may serve as an item of enhancement to the workout regimen. Bear in mind, however, there is a huge industry taking advantage of your investment. So be wise when choosing supplements.

Traveling in the Astral

The easiest missed component of the *Iron Alchemy* is sleep and it takes a particular kind of individual to enjoy it as something fruitful. It is the most powerful tool in the arsenal of body building and training. The changes that happen in your muscular system happen during the night; growth and adaptation. The goal of creating a better and stronger body happens when you sleep and nowhere else. Gateways are also opened to the mind that aren't accessible in waking life.

From a basic biological standpoint, large amounts of growth hormones are released while the body is sleeping. We can consider these small molecules the sweet nectar in the fruits of the gods. The science is very clear. Growth hormones play an important role in developing muscle mass. While it is true that the body also releases these during a workout, the majority of this happens while the body is at rest in the sleep state. (Some workouts like squats and deadlifts increase this amount dramatically, which is why we incorporate them and place such a heavy emphasis on them in the program.)

Besides being functional for the body's rejuvenation and growth, sleep can also be used as a practice for harnessing inward power. It is an occult window to another world. To do this practice the following every night.

As your body rests in suspended animation, envision the world as a decline into a valley.

Your waking hours were merely a descent into a foreign landscape. You were surrounded by mirages that distracted you from your own being. In a platonic sense, you were engulfed in the world of becoming. This world was the world of *Maya,* as described by the Indo-Europeans in the Vedic tradition.

As your eyes are closed, you are now inverting the world around you. The sun that shines in your chest is now awakened. It is in this place, the heart, that your true home resides.

The heart was known in ancient times as the seat of the soul. Because we are now so accustomed to experience life inside the brain, we have forgotten our very consiousness's origin and proper dwelling place.

Keep descending into a state of silence. As the fog of the mind dissipates, imagine yourself, or your consciousness as an entity of light. Practice moving it side to side, up and down, and then in a circular motion. Continue to do this until you feel an ease of movement and a detachment from the body.

Now when this is accomplished without struggle, begin to move your consciousness downward. It is important to note here, that one should not use their imagination with the 3d space of everyday life. Instead of moving vertically and feeling your descent with your body, use your imagination to feel it out. Use the imagination to discover the centers of the larynx and pharynx. Descend further, albeit, not vertically, until you find the heart.

Now that you are in your proper dwelling place, imagine yourself leaving the valley of the world. Waking life was a darkness. It was a memory you are now going to leave behind. Continue to leave behind the darkness. You are now entering the base of a new summit. This summit is where the gods reside.

Climb this summit, hand and foot. It is a mountain with the highest peak known to gods and men. Here is where the celestial fortress of Valhalla can be found. Leave the waking world behind and converse with the gods. In this place, true changes are made inward. Now let's move onto a practice that should be in place every night as you visit the astral realm.

Zach Bennet from Viking Fitness Climbs the Boulders of the Obed.

The mountain is one of the most important symbols in the Iron Alchemy. As such it should be a place where you visit, not only in meditation and dreams, but also in real life. You should go to mountains periodically and ritually. Here I stand upon the apex of Black Mountain in Crossville, Tennessee. I raise my horn to Odin and drink the mead.

Black Sun Exercise

"At night, before going to sleep, you should visualize a black sun rising in the west and traveling up into the sky, until it is directly overhead, as if it were noon. But remember, it's night time, so this sun isn't going to be hot or bright, but will possess properties entirely different than the sun that we're used to seeing.

Observe in your inner vision what this Black Sun looks like, what kind of radiation it gives off, what sort of feeling you get from it.

When you wake up the following morning, again bring the Black Sun to mind, only rather than seeing it rising, as the physical sun is rising, see it lowering from its zenith and descending beyond the eastern horizon."

- FROM THE YOGA OF POWER, BY JULIUS EVOLA

The ritual Julius Evola constructs in his *Yoga of Power* is simple, yet overwhelmingly powerful. It is very similar to the exercise we practiced in the previous pages.

The Black Sun is the true source of all self-knowledge. **Before we begin, we must take into consideration that this symbol has a different symbolism than that of the ordinary sun.**

The Black Sun was first discovered by the modern era when studying the migration patterns of the Alemanni and the vestiges that were left behind of their civilization. The symbol was worn on the brooches and belts of aristocrats in the Frankish and Alemanni tribes. The artifacts thus far discovered reveal many variations. In the specimens that have been found, the rays or spokes of the sun wheels consist of five to twelve *Sowilo* rays. Scholars debate the meaning of the number of spokes given, often attributing the number 12 to months of the year. However, all debaters consistently agree the symbol is connected to solar worship. However, solar worship would be incomplete without the attribute of power. Some of the specimens also embed a swastika in the middle of the sun.

The meaning of the Black Sun differs from that of the regular sun in a few profound ways. First, notice that it rises in the West, and such, it also sets in the East. It has a path reversed from that of its counterpart Sol. The Black Sun also comes out during the night, has its zenith at the darkest point in the night, and as it migrates it radiates no light into the surrounding darkness. This has purpose and meaning which I will disclose below.

The Black Sun's sole purpose is to eradicate lies and half-truths. As such it is not so much a harbinger of truth, as it is a weapon for the individual looking to clear the fog of the mind in error. If the sun reveals, then the function of the black sun is to devour. It opens the door to self-valuation, self-knowledge, and self-creation, and since initiations and old traditional support systems have dissipated with the sands of time, the black sun is a supreme symbol for the contemporary esoteric student.

Make note that the most powerful time to invoke the Black Sun is when all of life's certainties are wavering. As the light of truth becomes dim and beliefs are suspended. The fog created by erroneous thinking and misunderstandings can only be cleared by the use of this powerful symbol. Once invoked, however, there is no turning back from its power to destroy and its ability to create new pathways.

Using this exercise is crucial to gain true knowledge through experience, rather than digesting the beliefs of others. If you recall earlier in this book, all true knowledge comes through experience. However, this sort of illumination comes at its price – an internal struggle. All beliefs held prior will go through a crises. Assumptions will be questioned. Attachments will be discarded. The ending result however is the realization of what is true and what is false, which creates the need to obliterate realities that are false, and incompatible with your being.

And as always, true knowledge leads to liberation.

Picture: With a home-made torch I journey into the forest late at night. Such a ritual should be performed alone. It is a perfect reflection of the knowledge of the Black Sun in practice.

The Body as a Fortress

Our ancestors thought of Midgard as a fortress and an estate, as well as Asgard. That is why the ending "gard" was attached at the end of each of these words. These planes of existence were considered by our ancestors to be properties that must be secured and fortified. The same view must be reached about our bodies. We must take possession of them and then fortify them. They are the divine vessels that contain our noble souls.

If we are weak in one physical area, we must erect new walls and barriers for our upkeep. Sometimes we must scale back. *Like a sandcastle amidst the ocean's waves, smaller towers are taken out while the larger ones are better able to withstand the pulsating ocean.* For our bodies this means we must formulate strategies in our diet. If you are overweight you must learn to scale back the consumption of food. Your size is a weakness. If you are skinny, you must learn how to increase the size of your fortress. You are puny and therefore, weak and vulnerable. For the hard gainer, this means to eat. When full eat some more. *We are what we eat.*

This goes as much for the volume of our food consumption as it does the nutrients we are acquiring. Get them into your body. Quality is always preferred to quantity.

The fact of the matter is lifting weights is only part of the Iron Alchemy. If we imagine a pie chart, it consists of only a third of the entire process.

1/3 is nourishing the body
1/3 is training the body
1/3 resting the body

****None of these pieces are
more crucial than the other. ***

NOTE: All of this is only action based. These are only things we can do. However, these actions will never come to fruition if we do not first negotiate in ourselves what we truly are. *We are at war with the forces in the world that try to make us mundane.* Those primary forces are chaos and gravity! Our lives are a struggle to attain the divine nature that is seeded within us. This war, and the victory that comes from winning begins deep within our minds and hearts. If you cannot conquer within, then you will never be able to conquer outside reality. The holy battle is fought from within. The damned spirit of gravity is to be conquered inside, where it cannot penetrate, before it is conquered on the outside. The conspiracy is against you and all men. It seeks to reduce you into a primordial soup. Into a mass of nothingness.

Discipline is the tool that warriors use to ascend to the gods.

Chapter 5: Conclusion and the Meaning of the Iron Alchemy

Somewhere in the world there are men training. They are training to kill you. They are training to be better than you. They will overtake you when they get the chance. These men have not fallen for the lie that weakness is some kind of virtue to be admired.

Now the question stands... Are you prepared? The *Iron Alchemy* was written to prepare you for such a battle. It was written to prepare you against men and gods alike, for there are forces in the cosmos with consequences much more severe than man can create.

Preparation for any struggle begins by becoming strong. The stronger you are the harder you are to kill. As we train to become the elite warriors of our gods and our folk, we are transforming ourselves into a living and breathing rune of strength. Our runes of choice are *Uruz* and *Hagalaz*. With a deep understanding of how the runes work our mission is to become these two with no apologies or excuses. Our bodies will become reflections of our wills.

What is the lesson to be learned inside the contents of the *Iron Alchemy*? It is much more than a manifesto for fitness. Its mission is to bring about a crystallized a vision of the cosmos that is in alignment with the gods. Its esoteric leaning is to bring you about a path that can forge a pathway to the gods. The *Iron Alchemy* seeks for One-ness is to be obliterated. It is here to help reaffirm your existence as universalism seeks to plunge you into an abyss.

The predator never apologizes to its prey. Like so, you shall train. It is better to be strong than it is to be weak. Common sense will tell you that. A whole world in denial of the truth is still in denial. Do not fall for the lies propagated by the modern world and the never ending destruction of post-Christian morals. Furthermore, training is not a singular event. The gym, the history, the lore are not things to dabble in. They are a lifestyle that demands the allegiance of a warrior.

Despite the attempts of the politically correct in our society to write a narrative that is against our wills, we have realized that strength is to become something admired. To be strong is to wield something godly. It is a divine gift, but as the rune gebo has shown us, it is not earned without sacrifice.

Strength is difficult to obtain, and therefore, it is something that deserves your pride. In your heart, pride righteously sits in its throne.

With hard work and the right orientation, you can obtain all things. This book has given you the keys to unlock Odin's gates and enter his great halls.

Now is the time to join the ranks of the gods and heroes of the past. Train for Valhalla. Be prepared for Ragnarök.

Iron Alchemy is an act of rebellion against the contemporary world. It refuses to applaud weakness and ugliness. Instead it enshrines beauty and strength.

It is also part of our spiritual awakening that has been suppressed for over 1000 of years or more. Like the rune *Hagalaz,* Iron Alchemy is an act of destruction as well as an act of creation. It is an act of sacrifice, not only to the warrior gods of Asgard, but to you. Like Odin's great sacrifice to himself on the world tree, we sacrifice ourselves to ourselves. We also realize that there is no longer a place in this world for the individual driven by greed. Hedonism must be disposed of. The individual gets in the way of what you want and also degenerates the society we live in. To return to our roots we must honor transcendent values.

The Iron Alchemy is about acting out the struggle of life in a concrete way.

When we are engaged in crafting a body of the Gods we are also paying respect to the divine instrument that plays a role here in Midgard. No longer will we be horrified by ourselves, rejecting who we are. Instead, we see ourselves as beautified creations from the Gods who reign in the halls of Asgard. Yet, this divine perfection is not something inherited. It is merely a capacity given to us as a gift.

It is not a gift we reject. We train so we may earn it. We train so we may become strong. We train so that we may sit as equals with the Gods. Our goal is to inherit the Earth and a seat in…

VALHALLA.

Printed in Great Britain
by Amazon